CONTENTS

1

VERIFY ACCURACY

2

DISPUTES

3

CEASE AND DESIST

4

LATE PAYMENTS

This e-book will help you quickly repair your credit by providing simple steps and effective strategies to improve your credit score.

FOR THOSE WITH BAD CREDIT FOCUS ON:

- CHECKING YOUR CREDIT REPORT FOR ERRORS

- DISPUTE INACCURACIES, COLLECTIONS AND CHARGE OFFS

- NEGOTIATE A PAYMENT PLAN

- BUILD POSITIVE CREDIT HABITS FOR A FRESH START

3 STEPS TO CLEANING BAD CREDIT

1. CHECK YOUR CREDIT REPORT

START BY OBTAINING COPIES OF YOUR CREDIT REPORTS FROM ALL THREE MAJOR CREDIT BUREAUS:

EQUIFAX, EXPERIAN, AND TRANSUNION.

REVIEW EACH REPORT CAREFULLY FOR INACCURACIES, SUCH AS ACCOUNTS THAT DON'T BELONG TO YOU, INCORRECT LATE PAYMENTS, OR DEBTS THAT HAVE BEEN PAID BUT ARE STILL SHOWING AS OUTSTANDING.

2. DISPUTE ERRORS

IF YOU FIND ANY ERRORS ON YOUR CREDIT REPORTS, FILE A DISPUTE WITH THE CREDIT BUREAU REPORTING THE ERROR. YOU CAN USUALLY DO THIS ONLINE THROUGH THEIR WEBSITES.

PROVIDE ANY SUPPORTING DOCUMENTS THAT PROVE THE INFORMATION IS INCORRECT.

THE CREDIT BUREAU WILL INVESTIGATE THE DISPUTE AND EITHER CORRECT THE INFORMATION OR REQUEST VERIFICATION FROM THE CREDITOR.

THE CREDIT AGENCY IS SUPPOSE TO PROVIDE PROOF THAT THE DEBT WAS VERIFIED. REQUEST A COPY OF WHATEVER PROOF THEY OBTAINED TO VERIFY THE DEBT.

IF A DEBT HAS BEEN VERIFIED TWICE WITHOUT SHOWING VERIFIABLE PROOF AFTER IT WAS REQUESTED, FILE A COMPLAINT WITH THE CFPB AGAINST THE CREDIT AGENCY WHO DENIED REQUEST.

CONSUMER FINANCIAL PROTECTION BUREAU WEBSITE: CONSUMERFINANCE.GOV.

3. ADDRESS OUTSTANDING DEBTS

CREATE A PLAN TO TACKLE OUTSTANDING DEBTS. START BY PRIORITIZING DEBTS WITH THE HIGHEST INTEREST RATES OR THOSE THAT ARE CLOSEST TO BEING SENT TO COLLECTIONS.

ALWAYS NEGOTIATE ANY DEBT WITH THE ORIGINAL CREDITOR.

RECORD THE PHONE CALL OR HAVE THE CREDITOR EMAIL YOU A STATEMENT AGREEING TO DELETE CHARGE-OFF, ONCE YOU HAVE AGREED UPON A PAYMENT PLAN OR SETTLEMENT.

PAY TO DELETE

CONSIDER NEGOTIATING WITH CREDITORS FOR A SETTLEMENT OR PAYMENT PLAN IF YOU CANNOT PAY THE FULL AMOUNT.

VERIFY ACCURACY

UNDER THE FAIR CREDIT REPORTING ACT (FCRA), CONSUMERS HAVE RIGHTS WHEN IT COMES TO DISPUTING AND POTENTIALLY REMOVING COLLECTIONS AND CHARGE-OFFS FROM THEIR CREDIT REPORTS.

HERE ARE THE KEY FCRA LAWS THAT PERTAIN TO THESE ISSUES:

ACCURACY OF INFORMATION (SECTION 611):

THIS SECTION OF THE FCRA REQUIRES THAT CREDIT REPORTING AGENCIES (CRAS) MAINTAIN REASONABLE PROCEDURES TO ENSURE THE ACCURACY OF THE INFORMATION THEY REPORT. IF YOU BELIEVE THAT A COLLECTION OR CHARGE-OFF ON YOUR CREDIT REPORT IS INACCURATE OR INCOMPLETE, YOU HAVE THE RIGHT TO DISPUTE IT.

WHY YOU SHOULD VERIFY, NEGOTIATE, AND DISPUTE BEFORE MAKING PAYMENTS

BEFORE MAKING PAYMENTS ON DISPUTED ACCOUNTS, IT'S ESSENTIAL TO FOLLOW A STRATEGIC APPROACH OF VERIFYING, NEGOTIATING, AND DISPUTING.

1. VERIFICATION - ACCURACY:

VERIFYING THE ACCURACY OF THE DEBT ENSURES YOU'RE PAYING FOR LEGITIMATE OBLIGATIONS.

PREVENTS MISTAKES:

MISTAKES HAPPEN. VERIFYING PREVENTS YOU FROM PAYING FOR ERRORS OR DEBTS THAT ARE NOT YOURS.

LEGAL RIGHT: UNDER THE FAIR CREDIT REPORTING ACT (FCRA), YOU HAVE THE RIGHT TO REQUEST VERIFICATION OF ANY DEBT ON YOUR CREDIT REPORT.

2. NEGOTIATION

POTENTIAL SAVINGS:

NEGOTIATING ALLOWS YOU TO POTENTIALLY SETTLE FOR LESS THAN THE FULL AMOUNT OWED, SAVING YOU MONEY.
(ONLY WITH ORIGINAL CREDITOR)

PAYMENT TERMS:

NEGOTIATING PAYMENT TERMS CAN MAKE THE DEBT MORE MANAGEABLE AND PREVENT FINANCIAL STRAIN.

REMOVE NEGATIVE ITEMS:

SOMETIMES, NEGOTIATIONS INCLUDE AGREEMENTS TO REMOVE NEGATIVE ITEMS FROM YOUR CREDIT REPORT, IMPROVING YOUR SCORE.

3. **DISPUTE ERRORS:**

IF THERE ARE INACCURACIES IN THE DEBT REPORTING, DISPUTING ALLOWS YOU TO CORRECT THESE ERRORS.

LEGAL PROTECTION:

DISPUTING UNDER THE FCRA GIVES YOU LEGAL PROTECTION. CREDITORS AND CREDIT BUREAUS MUST INVESTIGATE AND VERIFY THE ACCURACY OF THE DEBT.

PRESERVE RIGHTS:

DISPUTING PRESERVES YOUR RIGHTS. IF THE DEBT CANNOT BE VERIFIED, IT MUST BE REMOVED FROM YOUR CREDIT REPORT.

BY FOLLOWING THIS APPROACH OF VERIFYING, NEGOTIATING, AND DISPUTING BEFORE MAKING PAYMENTS:

YOU ENSURE YOU'RE ONLY PAYING FOR VALID DEBTS.

YOU HAVE THE OPPORTUNITY TO SAVE MONEY THROUGH NEGOTIATION.

YOU PROTECT YOUR LEGAL RIGHTS UNDER THE FCRA.

YOU CAN POTENTIALLY REMOVE NEGATIVE ITEMS FROM YOUR CREDIT REPORT.

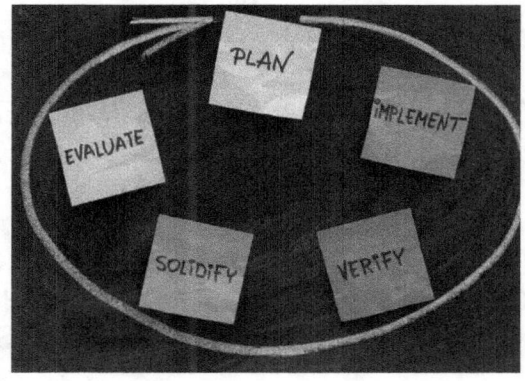

WHAT IS A COLLECTION?

A COLLECTION OCCURS WHEN A CREDITOR OR LENDER GIVES UP ON TRYING TO COLLECT PAYMENT FROM YOU DIRECTLY AND INSTEAD SELLS YOUR DEBT TO A THIRD-PARTY COLLECTION AGENCY. THIS AGENCY THEN BECOMES RESPONSIBLE FOR ATTEMPTING TO RECOVER THE DEBT FROM YOU. THE ORIGINAL CREDITOR MAY ALSO USE AN IN-HOUSE COLLECTIONS DEPARTMENT TO MANAGE THE DEBT.

COLLECTIONS TYPICALLY OCCUR WHEN YOU FAIL TO MAKE PAYMENTS ON A DEBT FOR AN EXTENDED PERIOD.

THE DEBT IS REPORTED TO CREDIT BUREAUS AS A COLLECTION ACCOUNT, WHICH CAN SIGNIFICANTLY IMPACT YOUR CREDIT SCORE.

COLLECTION AGENCIES MAY CONTACT YOU VIA MAIL, PHONE CALLS, OR EVEN LEGAL ACTION TO RECOVER THE DEBT.

RESOLVING COLLECTIONS CAN INVOLVE PAYING THE DEBT IN FULL, NEGOTIATING A SETTLEMENT FOR LESS THAN THE FULL AMOUNT, OR SETTING UP A PAYMENT PLAN.

I PERSONALLY WOULD NOT SUGGEST PAYING ANY THIRD PARTY COLLECTION AGENCIES.

ALWAYS CONTACT THE ORIGINAL DEBT COLLECTOR.

(I HAVE INCLUDED A SAMPLE VOICE SCRIPTS FOR WHEN CALLING THE CREDITOR)

WHAT IS A CHARGE-OFF?

A CHARGE-OFF HAPPENS WHEN A LENDER DETERMINES THAT A DEBT IS UNLIKELY TO BE COLLECTED AND WRITES IT OFF AS A LOSS. THIS DOESN'T MEAN YOU'RE OFF THE HOOK FOR THE DEBT; IT'S STILL OWED, BUT THE CREDITOR NO LONGER CONSIDERS IT A CURRENT ASSET.

A CHARGE-OFF TYPICALLY OCCURS AFTER YOU'VE BEEN DELINQUENT ON PAYMENTS FOR ABOUT 180 DAYS (6 MONTHS).

THE CREDITOR MAY CHOOSE TO SELL THE CHARGED-OFF DEBT TO A COLLECTION AGENCY, WHICH THEN PURSUES REPAYMENT.

LIKE COLLECTIONS, CHARGE-OFFS HAVE A SIGNIFICANT NEGATIVE IMPACT ON YOUR CREDIT SCORE.

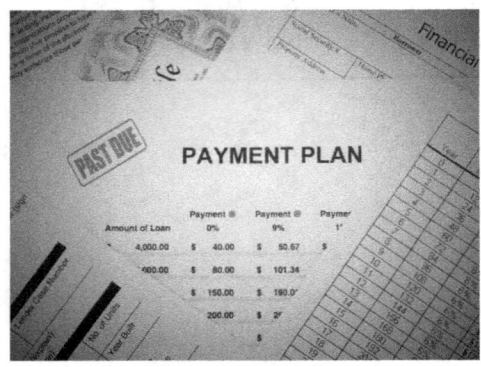

CHARGE OFFS AND COLLECTIONS TYPICALLY STAY ON YOUR CREDIT REPORT FOR UP TO SEVEN YEARS FROM THE DATE OF THE ORIGINAL DELINQUENCY.

IM GOING TO REPEAT, ALWAYS NEGOTIATE WITH THE ORIGINAL CREDITOR.

NEGOTIATING WITH THE ORIGINAL CREDITOR CAN BE MORE OF A ADVANTAGE BECAUSE THEY HAVE MORE AUTHORITY OVER THE TERMS OF YOUR DEBT.

THEY MAY OFFER MORE FLEXIBLE PAYMENT OPTIONS OR BE WILLING TO NEGOTIATE A SETTLEMENT THAT IS MORE FAVORABLE TO YOU.

ADDITIONALLY, RESOLVING THE DEBT WITH THE ORIGINAL CREDITOR MAY PREVENT FURTHER DAMAGE TO YOUR CREDIT REPORT.

A THIRD PARTY AGENCY HAS NO CONTROL OVER CLEARING PAST LATE PAYMENTS AND DELETING THE FULL NEGATIVE IMPACT OF THE ACCOUNT.

(SAMPLE LETTERS ON THE FOLLOWING PAGES CAN BE USED TO MAIL TO CREDIT BUREAUS)

SECTION 609 LETTER : DISPUTE OF INACCURATE INFORMATION

[YOUR NAME]
[YOUR ADDRESS]
[CITY, STATE ZIP CODE]
[DATE]

[CREDIT BUREAU NAME]
[CREDIT BUREAU ADDRESS]
[CITY, STATE ZIP CODE]

SUBJECT: DISPUTE OF INACCURATE INFORMATION - ACCOUNT NUMBER [YOUR ACCOUNT NUMBER]

DEAR SIR/MADAM,

I AM WRITING TO DISPUTE THE ACCURACY OF THE INFORMATION LISTED ON MY CREDIT REPORT UNDER ACCOUNT NUMBER [YOUR ACCOUNT NUMBER]. I BELIEVE THERE ARE INACCURACIES IN THE REPORTING OF THIS ACCOUNT, AND I AM REQUESTING AN INVESTIGATION AS ALLOWED UNDER SECTION 609 OF THE FAIR CREDIT REPORTING ACT.

SPECIFICALLY, I DISPUTE THE FOLLOWING INFORMATION:
- [DESCRIBE THE INACCURACIES, SUCH AS INCORRECT BALANCE, DATE OF LAST ACTIVITY, ETC.]

I REQUEST THAT YOU INVESTIGATE THESE DISCREPANCIES AND PROVIDE ME WITH THE RESULTS OF YOUR INVESTIGATION. IF THE INFORMATION IS FOUND TO BE INACCURATE, I ASK THAT IT BE CORRECTED OR REMOVED FROM MY CREDIT REPORT.

PLEASE CONDUCT THIS INVESTIGATION WITHIN 30 DAYS FROM THE DATE OF THIS LETTER AND PROVIDE ME WITH WRITTEN CONFIRMATION OF THE RESULTS.

SINCERELY,
[YOUR NAME]

THESE EXAMPLE LETTERS CAN BE USED FOR A SECTION 609 DISPUTE,.

FILL IN THE BLANKS:

HANDWRITE ALL PERSONAL AND ACCOUNT INFORMATION.

HANDWRITING THE FILL-IN BLANKS IN YOUR DISPUTE LETTER CAN INDEED INCREASE THE LIKELIHOOD OF YOUR LETTER BEING REVIEWED BY A REAL PERSON RATHER THAN PROCESSED BY AUTOMATED SYSTEMS. THIS PERSONAL TOUCH CAN POTENTIALLY LEAD TO A MORE THOROUGH INVESTIGATION OF YOUR DISPUTE AND A MORE EFFECTIVE RESOLUTION.

VERIFICATION OF DEBTS (SECTION 611):

IF YOU DISPUTE A COLLECTION ACCOUNT, THE CRA MUST VERIFY THE ACCURACY OF THE DEBT WITH THE ORIGINAL CREDITOR OR THE DEBT COLLECTOR. IF THEY CANNOT VERIFY THE DEBT, IT MUST BE REMOVED FROM YOUR CREDIT REPORT.

Dear Transunion,

The credit inquiries below are damaging to my credit rating. Please provide **full** documentation regarding the circumstances surrounding your release of my credit report pursuant to the permissible purpose provisions of the Fair Credit Reporting Act.

.
.
.

If you cannot provide such documentation, **you are obligated to remove the offending inquiry at once.**

Sincerely yours,

_____

TIME LIMIT FOR REPORTING (SECTION 605):

THE FCRA LIMITS THE AMOUNT OF TIME THAT NEGATIVE INFORMATION, SUCH AS COLLECTIONS AND CHARGE-OFFS, CAN REMAIN ON YOUR CREDIT REPORT. MOST NEGATIVE ITEMS CAN ONLY BE REPORTED FOR SEVEN YEARS FROM THE DATE OF THE DELINQUENCY THAT LED TO THE NEGATIVE ITEM. AFTER THIS TIME, THE ITEM MUST BE REMOVED.

SECTION 609 LETTER: REQUEST FOR VERIFICATION OF DEBT

[YOUR NAME]
[YOUR ADDRESS]
[CITY, STATE ZIP CODE]
[DATE]

[COLLECTION AGENCY NAME]
[COLLECTION AGENCY ADDRESS]
[CITY, STATE ZIP CODE]

SUBJECT: REQUEST FOR VERIFICATION OF DEBT - ACCOUNT NUMBER [YOUR ACCOUNT NUMBER]

DEAR SIR/MADAM,

I AM WRITING TO DISPUTE THE VALIDITY OF THE DEBT LISTED ON MY CREDIT REPORT UNDER ACCOUNT NUMBER [YOUR ACCOUNT NUMBER]. I AM REQUESTING VERIFICATION OF THIS DEBT AS ALLOWED UNDER SECTION 609 OF THE FAIR CREDIT REPORTING ACT.

I BELIEVE THERE MAY BE ERRORS OR INACCURACIES IN THE REPORTING OF THIS DEBT, AND I REQUEST THAT YOU PROVIDE ME WITH THE FOLLOWING INFORMATION:

1. THE ORIGINAL CREDITOR OF THE DEBT.
2. THE DATE OF THE LAST PAYMENT MADE ON THIS ACCOUNT.
3. A COMPLETE ACCOUNTING OF THE DEBT, INCLUDING ALL FEES, INTEREST, AND CHARGES.
4. ANY DOCUMENTATION RELATED TO THE DEBT, INCLUDING THE ORIGINAL SIGNED CONTRACT OR AGREEMENT.

PLEASE PROVIDE THIS INFORMATION TO ME WITHIN 30 DAYS FROM THE DATE OF THIS LETTER. IF YOU ARE UNABLE TO PROVIDE THE REQUESTED INFORMATION, I REQUEST THAT THIS DEBT BE REMOVED FROM MY CREDIT REPORT.

SINCERELY,
[YOUR NAME]

DISPUTES

DISPUTE PROCESS (SECTION 611):

WHEN YOU DISPUTE AN ITEM ON YOUR CREDIT REPORT, THE CRA MUST INVESTIGATE THE ITEM WITHIN 30 DAYS (EXTENDED TO 45 DAYS IF YOU SUBMIT ADDITIONAL INFORMATION DURING THE INITIAL 30-DAY PERIOD). THE CRA MUST ALSO PROVIDE YOU WITH THE RESULTS OF THE INVESTIGATION IN WRITING AND A FREE COPY OF YOUR UPDATED CREDIT REPORT IF THE DISPUTE RESULTS IN A CHANGE.

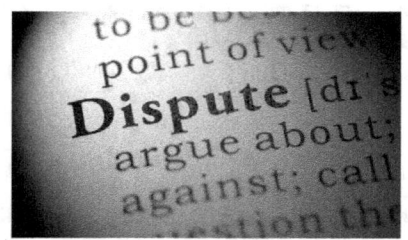

SUMMARY OF HOW CREDIT DISPUTES WORK:

CREDIT DISPUTES ALLOW CONSUMERS TO CHALLENGE INACCURACIES ON THEIR CREDIT REPORTS.

CONSUMERS CAN DISPUTE ERRORS SUCH AS INCORRECT ACCOUNT INFORMATION, LATE PAYMENTS, OR UNAUTHORIZED INQUIRIES.

(PHONE NUMBERS, ADDRESSES, WORK INFO)

GOODWILL DELETION:

CREDITORS OR COLLECTION AGENCIES MAY, AT THEIR DISCRETION, AGREE TO REMOVE A NEGATIVE ITEM FROM YOUR CREDIT REPORT AS A GOODWILL GESTURE.

THIS IS TYPICALLY DONE IF YOU HAVE A GOOD HISTORY OF ON-TIME PAYMENTS AND ARE SEEKING TO RESOLVE THE NEGATIVE ITEM.

IMPORTANT TIPS:

- BE CONCISE AND TO THE POINT

- STAY POLITE AND PROFESSIONAL THROUGHOUT THE CONVERSATION.

- TAKE NOTES DURING THE CALL, INCLUDING THE NAME OF THE PERSON YOU SPOKE WITH AND ANY KEY POINTS DISCUSSED.

- FOLLOW UP WITH A WRITTEN CONFIRMATION REQUEST AFTER THE CALL.

THIS SHORT SCRIPT IS DESIGNED TO QUICKLY PRESENT YOUR PAY-FOR-DELETE PROPOSAL AND GAUGE THE CREDITOR OR COLLECTION AGENCY'S WILLINGNESS TO PROCEED. REMEMBER TO ADJUST IT AS NEEDED FOR YOUR SPECIFIC SITUATION.

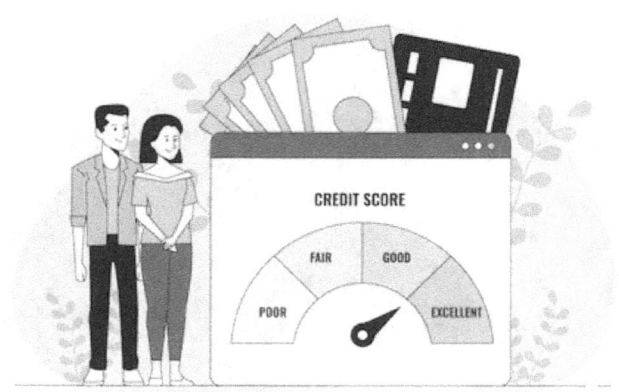

HERE'S A SHORT SCRIPT FOR A PAY-FOR-DELETE NEGOTIATION OVER THE PHONE:

HELLO, MY NAME IS [YOUR NAME], AND I'M CALLING ABOUT AN ACCOUNT WITH [CREDITOR OR COLLECTION AGENCY NAME] ON MY CREDIT REPORT.

PROPOSAL:
I WOULD LIKE TO DISCUSS A PAY-FOR-DELETE ARRANGEMENT FOR THIS ACCOUNT.
IF I MAKE A FULL PAYMENT OF [SPECIFY THE AMOUNT], WOULD YOU BE WILLING TO REMOVE THE NEGATIVE ITEM FROM MY CREDIT REPORT?

BENEFITS:
THIS WOULD HELP ME IMPROVE MY CREDIT SCORE AND FINANCIAL STANDING.
I BELIEVE IT WOULD BE MUTUALLY BENEFICIAL FOR US TO COME TO AN AGREEMENT.

CONFIRMATION AND DOCUMENTATION: CAN WE AGREE ON THIS ARRANGEMENT? IF SO, COULD YOU PROVIDE WRITTEN CONFIRMATION OF OUR AGREEMENT?
I'M PREPARED TO MAKE THE PAYMENT AS SOON AS WE HAVE A CLEAR AGREEMENT IN WRITING.

CLOSING:
THANK YOU FOR CONSIDERING MY PROPOSAL. I HOPE WE CAN COME TO A RESOLUTION THAT WORKS FOR BOTH OF US.

END OF SCRIPT

PAY-FOR-DELETE AGREEMENTS:

WHILE NOT SPECIFICALLY ADDRESSED IN THE FCRA, PAY-FOR-DELETE AGREEMENTS ARE SOMETIMES USED TO REMOVE COLLECTIONS FROM CREDIT REPORTS.

THIS IS A NEGOTIATION WHERE YOU AGREE TO PAY THE DEBT IN EXCHANGE FOR THE COLLECTION AGENCY REMOVING THE ITEM FROM YOUR REPORT. WHILE NOT GUARANTEED, SOME COLLECTION AGENCIES MAY AGREE TO THIS ARRANGEMENT.

(THIS LETTER CAN BE USED FOR PERSONAL USE JUST FILL IN THE BLANKS WHERE APPROPRIATE)

HERE'S AN EXAMPLE OF A PAY-FOR-DELETE LETTER THAT YOU CAN USE WHEN NEGOTIATING WITH A CREDITOR OR COLLECTION AGENCY TO HAVE A NEGATIVE ITEM REMOVED FROM YOUR CREDIT REPORT IN EXCHANGE FOR PAYMENT:

[YOUR NAME]
[YOUR ADDRESS]
[CITY, STATE ZIP CODE]
[DATE]

[COLLECTION AGENCY NAME]
[COLLECTION AGENCY ADDRESS]
[CITY, STATE ZIP CODE]

SUBJECT: PAY-FOR-DELETE AGREEMENT - ACCOUNT NUMBER [YOUR ACCOUNT NUMBER]

DEAR SIR/MADAM,

I AM WRITING TO DISCUSS THE POSSIBILITY OF ENTERING INTO A PAY-FOR-DELETE AGREEMENT REGARDING THE DEBT UNDER ACCOUNT NUMBER [YOUR ACCOUNT NUMBER]. I UNDERSTAND THAT THIS DEBT IS CURRENTLY LISTED AS A NEGATIVE ITEM ON MY CREDIT REPORT, AND I AM WILLING TO RESOLVE THIS MATTER BY MAKING PAYMENT IN FULL.

IN EXCHANGE FOR FULL PAYMENT OF THE DEBT, I AM REQUESTING THAT YOU REMOVE ALL NEGATIVE REFERENCES RELATED TO THIS ACCOUNT FROM MY CREDIT REPORTS WITH THE THREE MAJOR CREDIT BUREAUS: EQUIFAX, EXPERIAN, AND TRANSUNION. THIS INCLUDES ANY MENTION OF THE DEBT, AS WELL AS ANY LATE PAYMENTS OR OTHER DEROGATORY REMARKS.

I BELIEVE THAT A PAY-FOR-DELETE AGREEMENT WOULD BENEFIT BOTH PARTIES. BY RESOLVING THIS DEBT, I AM FULFILLING MY OBLIGATION, AND IN RETURN, THE NEGATIVE IMPACT ON MY CREDIT HISTORY WILL BE REMOVED.

PLEASE REVIEW THIS PROPOSAL AND LET ME KNOW IF YOU ARE WILLING TO PROCEED WITH A PAY-FOR-DELETE AGREEMENT. UPON YOUR ACCEPTANCE OF THIS PROPOSAL, I WILL PROMPTLY SUBMIT PAYMENT IN FULL VIA [METHOD OF PAYMENT].

I KINDLY REQUEST THAT YOU PROVIDE WRITTEN CONFIRMATION OF OUR AGREEMENT, INCLUDING THE TERMS OF THE PAY-FOR-DELETE ARRANGEMENT, FOR MY RECORDS. ONCE I RECEIVE THIS CONFIRMATION, I WILL PROCEED WITH THE PAYMENT AS AGREED.

THANK YOU FOR YOUR ATTENTION TO THIS MATTER. I LOOK FORWARD TO RESOLVING THIS ISSUE AMICABLY.

SINCERELY,
[YOUR NAME]

CEASE AND DESIST

CEASE COMMUNICATION REQUEST:

- YOU HAVE THE RIGHT TO REQUEST THAT A COLLECTION AGENCY CEASE COMMUNICATION WITH YOU REGARDING A DEBT.

- THE AGENCY MUST COMPLY WITH THIS REQUEST, BUT IT DOES NOT REMOVE THE DEBT FROM YOUR CREDIT REPORT.

YOU SHOULD FAMILIARIZE YOURSELF WITH YOUR RIGHTS UNDER THE FCRA AND FOLLOW THE PROPER STEPS WHEN DISPUTING NEGATIVE ITEMS ON YOUR CREDIT REPORT.

YES, YOU CAN POTENTIALLY SUE A DEBT COLLECTOR FOR CALLING AFTER A CEASE AND DESIST LETTER WAS SENT. VIOLATING A CEASE AND DESIST ORDER IS AGAINST THE LAW UNDER THE FAIR DEBT COLLECTION PRACTICES ACT (FDCPA). YOU MAY WANT TO CONSULT WITH A LAWYER WHO SPECIALIZES IN DEBT COLLECTION PRACTICES TO DISCUSS YOUR OPTIONS.

SECTION 609 LETTER: CEASE AND DESIST COMMUNICATION

[YOUR NAME]
[YOUR ADDRESS]
[CITY, STATE ZIP CODE]
[DATE]

[COLLECTION AGENCY NAME]
[COLLECTION AGENCY ADDRESS]
[CITY, STATE ZIP CODE]

SUBJECT: CEASE AND DESIST COMMUNICATION - ACCOUNT NUMBER [YOUR ACCOUNT NUMBER]

DEAR SIR/MADAM,

I AM WRITING TO REQUEST THAT YOU CEASE ALL COMMUNICATION WITH ME REGARDING THE DEBT UNDER ACCOUNT NUMBER [YOUR ACCOUNT NUMBER]. PURSUANT TO SECTION 609 OF THE FAIR CREDIT REPORTING ACT, I AM EXERCISING MY RIGHT TO REQUEST THAT YOU CEASE ALL COLLECTION ACTIVITIES.

I UNDERSTAND THAT YOU ARE REQUIRED TO COMPLY WITH THIS REQUEST, AND ANY FURTHER COMMUNICATION FROM YOUR AGENCY REGARDING THIS DEBT WILL BE CONSIDERED A VIOLATION OF THE FCRA.

PLEASE CONFIRM IN WRITING THAT YOU HAVE RECEIVED THIS REQUEST AND WILL CEASE ALL COMMUNICATION WITH ME REGARDING THIS DEBT.

SINCERELY,
[YOUR NAME]

FILL IN THE BLANKS:

HANDWRITE ALL PERSONAL AND ACCOUNT INFORMATION.

HANDWRITING THE FILL-IN BLANKS IN YOUR DISPUTE LETTER CAN INDEED INCREASE THE LIKELIHOOD OF YOUR LETTER BEING REVIEWED BY A REAL PERSON RATHER THAN PROCESSED BY AUTOMATED SYSTEMS. THIS PERSONAL TOUCH CAN POTENTIALLY LEAD TO A MORE THOROUGH INVESTIGATION OF YOUR DISPUTE AND A MORE EFFECTIVE RESOLUTION.

IMPORTANT NOTES:

- REPLACE [YOUR NAME], [YOUR ADDRESS], [CITY, STATE ZIP CODE], AND [YOUR ACCOUNT NUMBER] WITH YOUR ACTUAL INFORMATION.

- BE SURE TO INCLUDE THE SPECIFIC ACCOUNT NUMBER AND DETAILS RELATED TO THE DEBT.

- SEND THIS LETTER VIA CERTIFIED MAIL WITH RETURN RECEIPT REQUESTED TO HAVE PROOF OF DELIVERY.

- KEEP COPIES OF ALL CORRESPONDENCE FOR YOUR RECORDS.

- REMEMBER TO FOLLOW UP IF YOU DO NOT RECEIVE A RESPONSE WITHIN A REASONABLE TIMEFRAME.

LATE PAYMENTS

HOW LATE PAYMENTS CAN AFFECT YOUR CREDIT SCORE:

- LATE PAYMENTS CAN HAVE A SIGNIFICANT NEGATIVE IMPACT ON YOUR CREDIT SCORE.

- PAYMENT HISTORY IS THE MOST INFLUENTIAL FACTOR IN CALCULATING YOUR CREDIT SCORE, ACCOUNTING FOR ABOUT 35% OF THE TOTAL SCORE.

- A SINGLE LATE PAYMENT CAN CAUSE YOUR CREDIT SCORE TO DROP, ESPECIALLY IF IT IS REPORTED AS 30 DAYS OR MORE PAST DUE.

- THE MORE RECENT AND FREQUENT THE LATE PAYMENTS, THE GREATER THE NEGATIVE IMPACT ON YOUR SCORE.

- LATE PAYMENTS CAN STAY ON YOUR CREDIT REPORT FOR UP TO SEVEN YEARS.

- IT'S CRUCIAL TO MAKE ON-TIME PAYMENTS CONSISTENTLY TO MAINTAIN A GOOD CREDIT SCORE AND FINANCIAL HEALTH.

LATE PAYMENTS CAN SIGNIFICANTLY HARM YOUR CREDIT SCORE, MAKING IT HARDER TO QUALIFY FOR LOANS, CREDIT CARDS, AND FAVORABLE INTEREST RATES.

PHONE SCRIPT FOR NEGOTIATING LATE PAYMENTS:

INTRODUCTION:

- HELLO, MY NAME IS [YOUR NAME], AND I'M CALLING ABOUT LATE PAYMENTS ON MY ACCOUNT WITH [CREDITOR NAME] THAT ARE LISTED ON MY CREDIT REPORT.

ACKNOWLEDGMENT OF LATE PAYMENTS:

- I UNDERSTAND THAT THERE WERE LATE PAYMENTS ON MY ACCOUNT, AND I TAKE FULL RESPONSIBILITY FOR THOSE.
- HOWEVER, I AM WORKING ON IMPROVING MY CREDIT AND WOULD LIKE TO DISCUSS THE POSSIBILITY OF HAVING THOSE LATE PAYMENTS REMOVED FROM MY CREDIT REPORT.

EXPLANATION AND REQUEST:

- THE LATE PAYMENTS WERE DUE TO [EXPLAIN THE CIRCUMSTANCES, SUCH AS FINANCIAL HARDSHIP, A MISUNDERSTANDING, ETC.].
- I HAVE SINCE [DESCRIBE ANY ACTIONS TAKEN TO IMPROVE FINANCIAL STABILITY, SUCH AS MAKING ON-TIME PAYMENTS, CREATING A BUDGET, ETC.].
- I AM REQUESTING THAT THE LATE PAYMENTS BE REMOVED FROM MY CREDIT REPORT TO HELP ME REBUILD MY CREDIT.

BENEFITS OF REMOVAL:

- REMOVING THESE LATE PAYMENTS WOULD SIGNIFICANTLY IMPROVE MY CREDIT SCORE AND FINANCIAL STANDING.
- IT WOULD ALSO DEMONSTRATE MY COMMITMENT TO RESPONSIBLE FINANCIAL MANAGEMENT.

CONFIRMATION AND DOCUMENTATION:

- CAN WE DISCUSS THE POSSIBILITY OF REMOVING THESE LATE PAYMENTS FROM MY CREDIT REPORT?
- IF WE CAN COME TO AN AGREEMENT, I WOULD LIKE TO REQUEST WRITTEN CONFIRMATION OF THE REMOVAL AND THE UPDATED CREDIT REPORT.

CLOSING:

- THANK YOU FOR CONSIDERING MY REQUEST. I BELIEVE REMOVING THESE LATE PAYMENTS WOULD BE BENEFICIAL FOR BOTH PARTIES.
- PLEASE LET ME KNOW IF WE CAN WORK TOGETHER ON THIS, AND IF THERE'S ANY ADDITIONAL INFORMATION YOU NEED FROM ME.

END OF SCRIPT

[YOUR NAME]
[YOUR ADDRESS]
[CITY, STATE, ZIP CODE]
[YOUR EMAIL ADDRESS]
[YOUR PHONE NUMBER]
[DATE]

[CREDIT BUREAU NAME]
[CREDIT BUREAU ADDRESS]
[CITY, STATE, ZIP CODE]

SUBJECT: DISPUTE OF INACCURATE LATE PAYMENT REPORTING

DEAR SIR/MADAM,

I AM WRITING TO DISPUTE THE LATE PAYMENT REPORTED ON MY CREDIT REPORT. ACCORDING TO THE FAIR CREDIT REPORTING ACT (FCRA), SECTION 611, CONSUMERS HAVE THE RIGHT TO DISPUTE INACCURATE INFORMATION ON THEIR CREDIT REPORTS.

UPON REVIEWING MY CREDIT REPORT, I NOTICED A LATE PAYMENT REPORTED FOR THE ACCOUNT WITH THE FOLLOWING DETAILS:

CREDITOR NAME: [NAME OF CREDITOR]
ACCOUNT NUMBER: [ACCOUNT NUMBER, IF AVAILABLE]
DATE OF LATE PAYMENT: [DATE OF LATE PAYMENT]
AMOUNT OF LATE PAYMENT: [AMOUNT OF LATE PAYMENT]

I BELIEVE THIS LATE PAYMENT IS INACCURATE FOR THE FOLLOWING REASONS:

1. [EXPLAIN ANY DISCREPANCIES OR ERRORS IN THE REPORTING OF THE LATE PAYMENT, SUCH AS INCORRECT DATE, AMOUNT, OR ACCOUNT INFORMATION.]

CONTINUED...

2. [PROVIDE ANY ADDITIONAL INFORMATION OR CIRCUMSTANCES THAT SUPPORT YOUR DISPUTE, SUCH AS EVIDENCE OF TIMELY PAYMENT OR EXTENUATING CIRCUMSTANCES.]

AS PER THE FCRA, I REQUEST THAT YOU CONDUCT A THOROUGH INVESTIGATION INTO THE ACCURACY OF THE LATE PAYMENT REPORTING AND REMOVE IT FROM MY CREDIT REPORT IF IT CANNOT BE VERIFIED. I ALSO REQUEST THAT YOU PROVIDE ME WITH A COPY OF MY UPDATED CREDIT REPORT ONCE THE INVESTIGATION IS COMPLETE.

ENCLOSED ARE COPIES OF SUPPORTING DOCUMENTATION, INCLUDING [LIST ANY DOCUMENTATION SUPPORTING YOUR DISPUTE, SUCH AS PAYMENT RECORDS, CORRESPONDENCE WITH THE CREDITOR, OR ANY OTHER RELEVANT EVIDENCE].

SINCERELY,
[YOUR NAME]

Conclusion

USING 609 AND 611 LETTERS WILL HELP IMPROVE CREDIT SCORE. PRACTICE RESPONSIBLE CREDIT USE, DIVERSIFYING CREDIT TYPES, AND KEEPING CREDIT UTILIZATION LOW.

Here are the phone numbers and addresses for the three major credit bureaus:

1. Equifax:
- Phone Number: 1-866-349-5191
- Address: Equifax Information Services LLC, P.O. Box 740241, Atlanta, GA 30374-0241

2. Experian:
- Phone Number: 1-888-397-3742
- Address: Experian, P.O. Box 4500, Allen, TX 75013

3. TransUnion:
- Phone Number: 1-800-916-8800
- Address: TransUnion LLC, P.O. Box 2000, Chester, PA 19016

BIOGRAPHY

"IN THIS EMPOWERING EBOOK, I'VE SHARED WITH YOU THE KEYS TO UNLOCK A WORLD OF FINANCIAL FREEDOM AND PROSPERITY.

AS A SEASONED EXPERT IN THE REALM OF CREDIT MANAGEMENT, I'VE DEDICATED MY CAREER TO GUIDING INDIVIDUALS LIKE YOU TOWARDS A BRIGHTER FINANCIAL FUTURE.

GET READY TO EMBARK ON A JOURNEY OF SELF-DISCOVERY, EMPOWERMENT, AND LASTING PROSPERITY."

—ANTONIONIA MARIE